# GEOFFREY BUSH

# Christmas Cantata

for soprano solo, SATB, string orchestra & oboe obbligato

Order No: NOV 070070

NOVELLO PUBLISHING LIMITED

# A CHRISTMAS CANTATA

Lullay, Jesu, Lullay.

O God, forasmuch as without thee we are not able to please thee; Mercifully grant, that thy Holy Spirit may in all things direct and rule our hearts; through Jesus Christ our Lord. *Amen.*

*Collect for the Nineteenth Sunday after Trinity.*

## II

The first good joy that Mary had,
It was the joy of one ;
To see the blessèd Jesus Christ,
When He was first her son.
  *When He was first her son, good man,*
  *And blessèd may He be.*
  *Praise Father, Son and Holy Ghost,*
  *To all eternity.*

The next good joy that Mary had,
It was the joy of two ;
To see her own son, Jesus Christ,
To make the lame to go.
  *To make the lame to go, good man,*
  *And blessèd may He be.*
  *Praise Father, Son and Holy Ghost,*
  *To all eternity.*

The next good joy that Mary had,
It was the joy of three ;
To see her own son, Jesus Christ,
To make the blind to see.
  *To make the blind to see, good man,*
  *And blessèd may He be.*
  *Praise Father, Son and Holy Ghost,*
  *To all eternity.*

The next good joy that Mary had,
It was the joy of four ;
To see her own son, Jesus Christ,
To read the Bible o'er.
  *To read the Bible o'er, good man,*
  *And blessèd may He be.*
  *Praise Father, Son and Holy Ghost,*
  *To all eternity.*

The next good joy that Mary had,
It was the joy of five ;
To see her own son, Jesus Christ,
To bring the dead alive.
　　*To bring the dead alive, good man,*
　　*And blessèd may He be.*
　　*Praise Father, Son and Holy Ghost,*
　　*To all eternity.*

The next good joy that Mary had,
It was the joy of six ;
To see her own son, Jesus Christ,
Upon the crucifix.
　　*Upon the crucifix, good man,*
　　*And blessèd may He be.*
　　*Praise Father, Son and Holy Ghost,*
　　*To all eternity.*

The next good joy that Mary had,
It was the joy of seven ;
To see her own son, Jesus Christ,
To wear the crown of heaven.
　　*To wear the crown of heaven, good man,*
　　*And blessèd may He be.*
　　*Praise Father, Son and Holy Ghost,*
　　*To all eternity.   Amen.*

Traditional.

## III

When Jesus Christ was four years old,
The Angels brought Him toys of gold,
Which no man ever had bought or sold.

And yet with these He would not play,
He made Him small fowl out of clay,
And blest them till they flew away.
　　*Tu creasti, Domine.*

Jesus Christ, Thou child so wise,
Bless mine hands and fill mine eyes,
And bring my soul to Paradise.

Hilaire Belloc.

(*By permission of Messrs. Gerald Duckworth & Co. Ltd.*)

## IV

Little Jesus, sweetly sleep, do not stir ;
We will lend a coat of fur ;
We will rock you, rock you, rock you,
We will rock you, rock you, rock you :
See the fur to keep you warm,
Snugly round your tiny form.

Mary's little baby, sleep, sweetly sleep,
Sleep in comfort, slumber deep ;
We will rock you, rock you, rock you,
We will rock you, rock you, rock you :
We will serve you all we can ;
Darling, darling little man.

*Translated from a Czech Carol by Percy Dearmer.*

(*Printed by permission of the Oxford University Press*)

## V

Rejoice !
O make we merry, both more and less,
For now is the time of Christemas.

Let no man come into this hall,
Nor groom, nor page, nor yet marshall,
But that some sport he bring withal.

If that he say he cannot sing,
Some other sport then let him bring,
That it may please at this feasting.

If that he say he naught can do,
Then for my love, ask him no moe,
But into the stocks then let him go.

O make we merry, both more and less,
For now is the time of Christemas.

*c.* 1500.

# VI

This endris night I saw a sight,
A star as bright as day ;
And ever among a maiden sung,
By by, lully, lullay.

This lovely Lady sat and sung,
And to her child did say,
" My son, my brother, father dear,
Why liest thou thus in hay ?

" My sweetest bird, thus 'tis required,
Though thou be King veray,
But none the less, I will not cease
To sing, By, by, lullay."

*15th century.*

# VII

I sing of a maiden
  That is makeles ;
King of all kings
  To her son she ches.

He came all so still
  There his mother was,
As dew in April
  That falleth on the grass.

He came all so still
  To his mother's bour,
As dew in April
  That falleth on the flour.

He came all so still
  There his mother lay,
As dew in April
  That falleth on the spray.

Mother and maiden
  Was never none but she ;
Well may such a lady
  Goddes mother be.

*15th century.*

# VIII

*By by lullay, thou little tiny child,*
*By by, lully, lullay.*

O sisters too,
How may we do
   For to preserve this day
This poor youngling,
For whom we sing,
   *By by, lully, lullay ?*

Herod the king
In his raging,
   Chargèd he hath this day
His men of might,
In his own sight,
   All children young to slay.

Then woe is me,
Poor child, for thee,
   And ever, morn and day,
For thy parting
Ne say nor sing
   *By by, lully, lullay.*

            *15th century.*

# IX

I saw three ships come sailing in,
   *On Christmas day, on Christmas day,*
I saw three ships come sailing in,
   *On Christmas day in the morning.*

And what was in those ships all three ?
Our Saviour Christ and his Lady.
Pray whither sailed those ships all three ?
O, they sailed into Bethlehem.
And all the bells on earth shall ring,
And all the angels in heav'n shall sing.
   *Rejoice on Christmas Day in the morning.*

            *Traditional.*

## Epilogue

The grace of our Lord Jesus Christ, and the love of God, and the fellowship of
the Holy Ghost, be with us all evermore. *Amen.*

            *2 Cor. XIII.*

# CONTENTS

Nos. 2, 4, 6, 8 and 9 are based on traditional carol tunes.

All the movements except the first and the last may be performed separately. If a shortened version of the cantata is required, the following selection of movements should be used :—Nos. 1, 2, 3, 4 or 6 (but not both), 7 and 9.

Full Score and Orchestral parts are available on hire, also an arrangement of the accompaniment for Oboe and Piano.

Time of performance approximately 35 minutes.

# A CHRISTMAS CANTATA

## for Soprano Solo, Chorus, Oboe and String Orchestra

GEOFFREY BUSH

*For A. R. McD. G.*

## I. PRELUDE

2

**7**

CHORUS. SOPRANO
**Tempo I**
*mp molto tranquillo*

Lul - lay_ Je - su, Lul - lay_
*p molto tranquillo*

Je - su, Lul - lay_ Je - su, Lul - lay_ Je - su, Lul - lay_

**8**

Je - su, Lul - lay_ Je - su, Lul - lay_ Je - su,

Lul - lay_ Je - su, Lul - lay_ Je - su, Lul - lay_

*pp teneramente*

Je-su, Lul - lay_ Je-su, Lul - lay_ Je-su,

Lul - lay_ Je-su, Lul - lay_ Je-su, Lul - lay_

(SOPRANO) Je - su, Lul - lay._

TENOR & BASS mp

* O God, forasmuch as without thee we are not able to

(TENOR & BASS) please thee; Mercifully grant, that thy Holy Spirit may in all things direct and rule our hearts; through Je - sus Christ our

*All or part of the collect for Christmas Day may be used here if preferred.

17362

# II. THE SEVEN JOYS OF MARY

## Theme and Variations

poco rit.

_mp_

Fa - ther, Son and Ho - ly Ghost, To all e - ter - ni - ty. The

_mf_
_poco a poco dim._

poco rit.

**14** VAR. I
**a tempo**

_tranquillo_

next good joy that Ma - ry had, It was the joy of

_mp tranquillo_

two; To see her own son,— Je - sus Christ, To

make the lame to go. To make the lame to—

Fa-ther, Son and Ho-ly Ghost, To all e-ter-ni-

TENOR & BASS **15** VAR. II

*mf con brio*

-ty. The next good joy that Ma-ry had, It was the joy of

three; To see her own son, Je-sus Christ, To make the blind to

*cresc.*

9

17362

see. To make the blind to— see, good man, And bless-ed may He

be. Praise Fa - ther, Son and Ho - ly Ghost, To all e - ter - ni -

SOPRANO & ALTO **16** VAR. III
*mp* *commodo*

- ty. The next good joy that Ma - ry had, It was the joy of

four; To see her own son, Je - sus Christ, To read the Bi - ble

o'er. To read the Bi - ble o'er, good man, And bless-ed may He

be. Praise Fa - ther, Son and Ho - ly Ghost, To all e - ter - ni-

TENOR & BASS **17** VAR. IV
*mf* *energico*

-ty. The next good joy that Ma - ry had, It

*f energico*

was the joy of five; To see her own son,—

8 - - - - - - - -

Praise Fa-ther, Son and Ho-ly Ghost, To all e - ter - ni - ty.

next good joy that Ma-ry had, It was the joy of seven; To

The next good joy that Ma-ry had, It was the joy of

## III. WHEN JESUS CHRIST WAS FOUR YEARS OLD

### Chorale

Words by Hilaire Belloc*

For G.P.G.

# IV. LITTLE JESUS, SWEETLY SLEEP
### Lullaby

Words translated from a Czech Carol
by Percy Dearmer

22

# V. MAKE WE MERRY BOTH MORE AND LESS

## Scherzo

*Precision and attack are all-important in this Scherzo. If intonation gives trouble, a little instrumental support may be given as a last resort.

now is the time of Christ - e - mas, For now is the time of

Now's the time of Christ - e - mas, For now is the time of

Now's the time of Christ - e - mas, For now is the time of

Now's the time of Christ - e - mas, For now is the time of

Christ - e - mas. O let us re - joice, re - joice, re-joice. O let us re -

Christ - e - mas. Re - joice, re - joice, re-joice. Re -

Christ - e - mas. O let us re - joice, re - joice, re-joice. O let us re -

Christ - e - mas. Re - joice, re - joice, re-joice. Re -

30

this feast-ing. O let us re - joice, re - joice, re-joice, O let us re - joice, re -

32

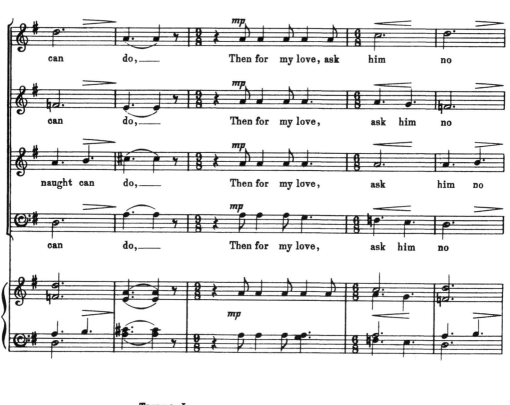

38

17362

*For J. N. B.*

# VI. THIS ENDRIS NIGHT I SAW

Carol

CHORUS. TENOR & BASS

This end - ris night I saw a sight, A
star as bright as day; And ev - er a - mong a maid - en sung, By

by, lul-ly, lul - lay, sung, lul-ly, lul - lay. This

**39 pochissimo più mosso**
SOPRANO & ALTO

love - ly La - dy sat and sung, And to her child _ did

say, _____ "My son, my bro-ther, fa - ther dear, Why

liest thou thus in hay?

* = true

By by, By by, lul - ly, lul - lay.

*Omit the A unless it can be sung easily

For D.R.C.B.

# VII. I SING OF A MAIDEN
## Intermezzo

\* = matchless
† = chose

46

He came all so still _____ There his mo-ther

lay, _____ As dew in A - pril That

fall - eth on the spray. _____

Mo - ther and maid - en

For D.G.M.

## VIII. BY BY LULLAY, THOU LITTLE TINY CHILD

Lament

52

17362

**52**

might, In his own sight, All children young to slay.

might, In his own sight, All children young to slay.

He-rod, He-rod, King He-rod, He-rod,

He-rod, He-rod, King He-rod, He-rod,

**52**

He-rod, He-rod,

He-rod, He-rod, He-rod,

He-rod, He-rod, He-rod,

He-rod, He-rod, He-rod,

# IX. FINALE. I SAW THREE SHIPS

followed by Epilogue

Christmas day, on Christmas day, on Christmas day, Re - joice.

Christmas day, on Christmas day, on Christmas day, Re - joice.

Christmas day, on Christmas day, on Christmas day, Re - joice.

I saw three ships come

57

57

17362

58

17362

ships all three, On Christmas day, on Christmas day, Pray whith - er sailed those

*mp* **62**

O, they sailed in - to

ships all three, On Christmas day in the morn - ing?

**62**

Beth - le - hem, On Christmas day, on Christmas day, O, they sailed in - to

Beth - le - hem, to Beth - le - hem, to Beth - le - hem to Beth - le - hem,

*mp*

*p*

*più p*

62

64

64

17362

**69** EPILOGUE
Con moto, agitato

CHORUS. TENOR & BASS

The grace of our Lord Jesus Christ, and
the love of God, and the fellowship of the
Holy Ghost, be with us all evermore.  } A - men.

**70** *CHORUS.* SOPRANO
*dolcissimo*

Lul - lay_ Je-su, lul - lay_ Je-su, lul - lay_

poco rit.  a tempo, più tranquillo

Je-su._

68

Printed and bound in Great Britain by
Caligraving Limited Thetford Norfolk